A Child's First Library of Learning

Things to Do

TIME-LIFE BOOKS • ALEXANDRIA, VIRGINIA

Contents

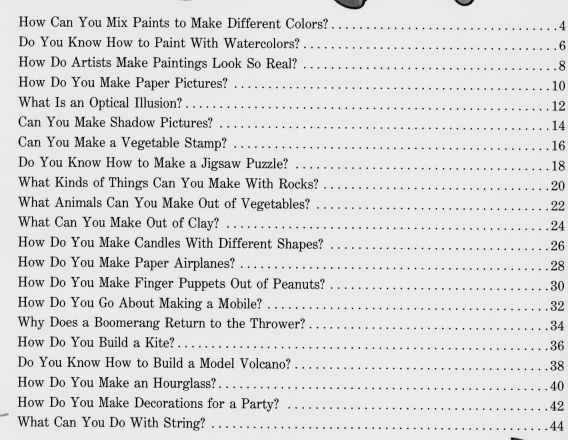

❓ How Can You Mix Paints To Make Different Colors?

ANSWER You must start with the red, blue and yellow. These three are called the primary colors. When you mix them in different amounts you can make all the colors in the rainbow. Why not try mixing these colors yourself? See if you can make the colors you see on the next page.

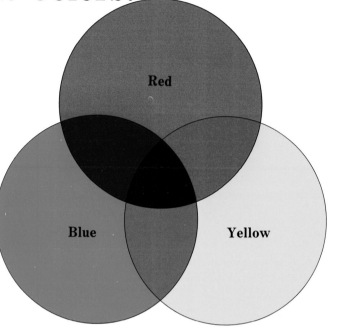

■ Colors in a photo

This photo is made up of yellow, red, blue and black dots, as you can see below. If you use a powerful magnifying glass you can see the small dots.

Mixing the three primary colors

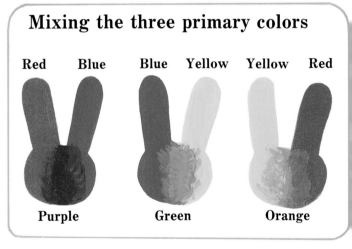

Red   Blue   Blue   Yellow   Yellow   Red

Purple   Green   Orange

▼ **Yellow dots**   ▼ **Red dots**   ▼ **Blue dots**   ▼ **Black dots**

4

What Can We Do With Just Two Colors?

When artists paint pictures they often use a lot of different colors. They can do this by changing the amount of one color of paint that's mixed with another. Painters can make a color lighter by adding white to it. When the lightness or darkness of a color is changed we can call the new color a shade.

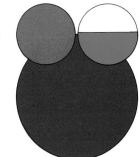

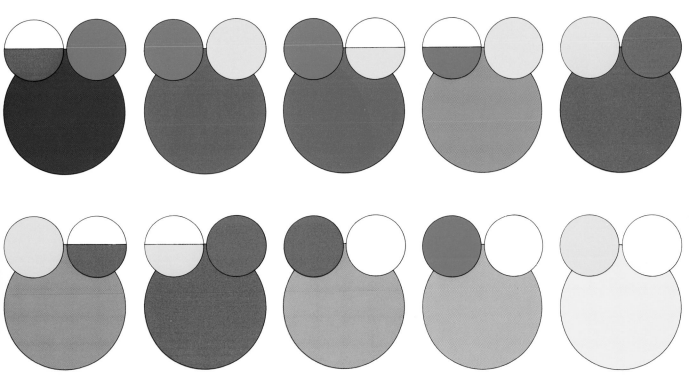

Be sure to use the colors before they dry

The colors won't blend and the jar won't look real if you paint on top of a color that has dried.

If you add the second color before the first has dried they blend, making the jar look real.

● To the Parent

Painting with watercolors is an activity that most children enjoy. It is the first of dozens of things to do that your child will discover in this book. Some of the things in this book can be done by very young children, while other pages have more challenging activities, which are designed for older readers. A few activities require some adult supervision. We suggest that you review this book with your child. We consider parents the best judges of which activities will be most suitable for their children.

Do You Know How to Paint With Watercolors?

ANSWER Some paints are made to be mixed with water. When you make a picture with them use water to spread the color. This is one of many ways to paint. Why not try the ones you see on the next page?

■ Materials

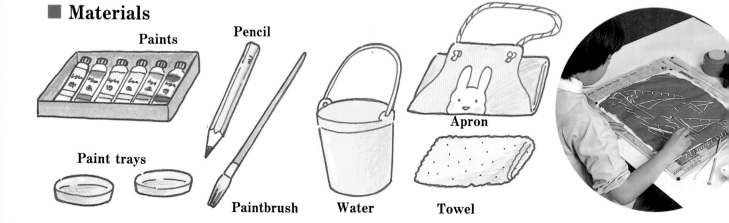

Paints

Pencil

Apron

Paint trays

Paintbrush

Water

Towel

How should I use watercolors?

It's best to use a pencil first. Make an outline of your picture. Be sure to include all the important parts. Don't press too hard.

Wet your brush. Begin by using the light colors. Wash your brush before you use another color.

After you have painted with the light colors, add the darker colors. Be sure to fill in all the highlights.

Here are some other ways to paint

Squeeze some paint on paper and use a triangle or ruler to spread it.

Trace lots of lines through the paint with a comb or toothbrush.

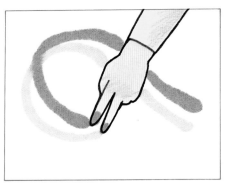

Try finger painting. You can mix paste or flour in with your paint.

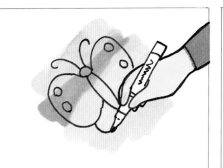

First paint a pattern very lightly, then use a felt-tipped pen to add the details after the paint has dried.

Use just the tip of a paintbrush and draw a shape using dots only. You can also use a pencil or felt-tipped pen.

Try using odd-shaped things like some vegetable peel, cotton wool or old rubber toys to make patterns.

Always clean up afterward

Be sure to wash out your paintbrush and paint trays. If you leave paint in them it will harden. And remember always to paint in old clothes or with an apron on.

How Do Artists Make Paintings Look So Real?

ANSWER People like to paint pictures of things they see. But sometimes it is hard making your picture look very real. Artists know how to make pictures look right. They have learned certain tricks that help them do this.

Draw a friend's face. Look carefully to see the special features in that person's face.

When drawing someone's face, first make an outline. Then position the eyes and nose. When making a sketch it may help to use center lines. And remember that most shapes are curved.

■ Change the horizon

The horizon is a line where the sky meets land or water. Its position makes things seem near or far, or large or small.

■ Determine the size

Which picture do you think looks more realistic? To create depth, nearer objects should be drawn larger. Objects that are farther away should be drawn smaller.

The scene looks different if you change the position of the horizon. When drawing scenery you should pay close attention to the size of objects that are near or far away.

● To the Parent

Perspective and proportion are difficult even for adults to render realistically in drawings. Children, especially younger children, tend to draw their main subjects larger than they actually appear. In teaching children to draw encourage them to take a good look at a scene first. If possible have them touch the subject before attempting to draw it. When drawing human figures, modeling with clay helps them better understand the body's true shape and proportions. When you critique a child's work be positive and use statements like, "That's a beautiful color," or "This is a good curve." A trip to a museum or art gallery is a good way to teach children about art.

❓ How Do You Make Paper Pictures?

ANSWER You can make wonderful pictures by cutting up colorful paper. Use paper you find around the house. Look for construction paper, wrapping paper or tissue paper. Ask your parents if you can use old newspapers or magazines. One way to make pictures is to draw an outline in pencil. Then you cut paper to fit the outline. It's also fun to take odd shapes and sizes and to mix them in creative ways. This kind of picture is called a collage.

■ Materials

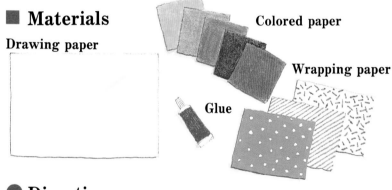

Drawing paper

Colored paper

Wrapping paper

Glue

● Directions

Start by making a rough sketch on a piece of paper. Don't try to draw too much detail. If you already have some torn pieces of paper, you might think of something interesting to make with them.

Cut the paper into the sizes and shapes you need. Scissors will be helpful, but you can also make interesting shapes by tearing the paper by hand.

Before you paste the pieces of paper together, put the picture together in different ways. How does it look best? When the paste is dry you can add important details with paints, pencils or crayons.

▲ With some colored paper you can make a cat.

10

▲ Wavy black paper on white will produce a zebra.

Making Sand Paintings

■ Materials

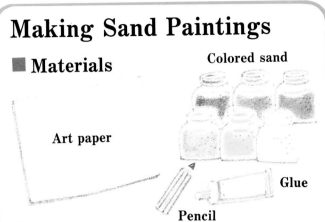

Art paper

Colored sand

Pencil

Glue

● Directions

First draw a picture on the paper. Next decide the colors you will need and where you will put them. When you make a picture with sand you start with the darkest color. Carefully put glue on the paper everywhere the first color will go. Sprinkle the sand over the glue and let it dry a bit. Brush or shake the extra sand from the picture and then put glue on the paper for the next color. Don't hurry. You need to take your time when you're working with sand and glue. Add only one color at a time. When you have finished put the picture in a safe place and leave it there until it has dried completely.

◀ First draw your design in pencil.

When you add the ▶ sand, start with the darkest color.

• To the Parent

The activities described here will help encourage the child to think about size, shape and color. Sand and colored paper also help introduce the idea of texture. Cutting out paper shapes, especially when a child first draws an outline, also promotes the development of motor skills. Children love to tell stories about the pictures they create, and this is a good way for them to exercise their imagination. A series of pictures can be used to illustrate a long story such as a fairy tale or legend.

11

What Is an Optical Illusion?

ANSWER Sometimes your eyes can play tricks on you. For example an object by itself may appear to be one size when you look at it. When you see it in comparison to other things it suddenly seems to be bigger or smaller. We call this trick an optical illusion.

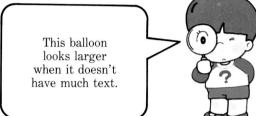

This balloon looks larger when it doesn't have much text.

■ **Which cookie do you think is bigger?**

The cookies in the middle of each batch are actually the same size!

12

■ Which is larger?

The center lines are both the same length.

Which boy do you think looks taller? They're the same height actually. Are you surprised?

■ What do they look like?

Turned upside-down, what happens?

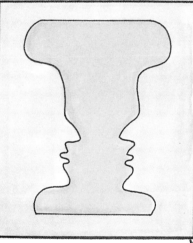

Is it a vase or two faces?

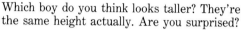

Are the crosses light or dark?

What's going on? Strange things seem to be happening in these pictures. Are our eyes fooling us?

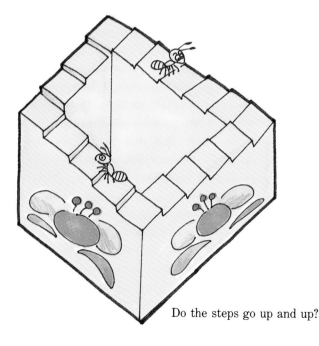

Do the steps go up and up?

13

?Can You Make Shadow Pictures?

ANSWER Whenever you are in the light you cast a shadow. A shadow is usually the same shape as the object that casts it. Objects that are colored and allow light to pass through them cast shadows of that color. You can make shadow puppets of cats and dogs with your hands or cut out shadow puppets from paper. If you darken a room and cast shadows on a thin white cloth or paper from behind, you can make your own shadow puppet theater.

▲ These shadow puppets were created with empty bottles.

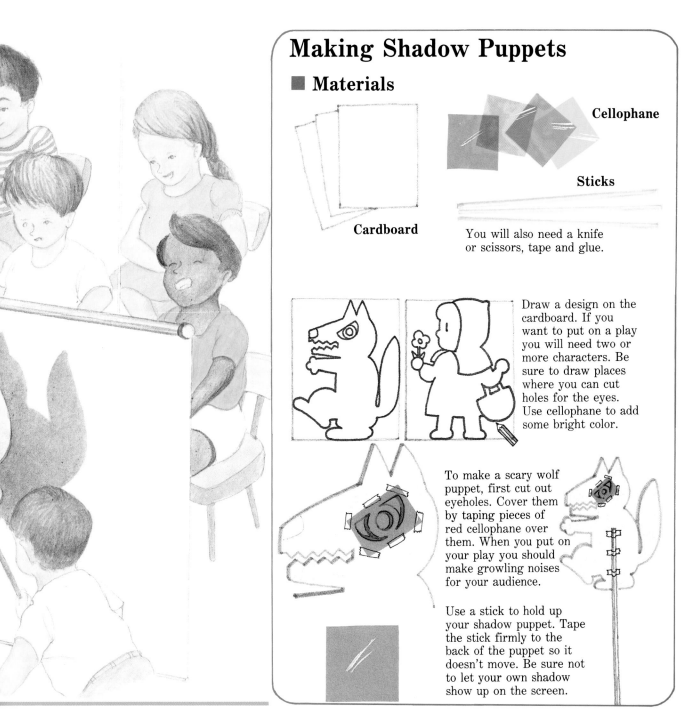

Making Shadow Puppets

■ Materials

Cellophane

Sticks

Cardboard

You will also need a knife or scissors, tape and glue.

Draw a design on the cardboard. If you want to put on a play you will need two or more characters. Be sure to draw places where you can cut holes for the eyes. Use cellophane to add some bright color.

To make a scary wolf puppet, first cut out eyeholes. Cover them by taping pieces of red cellophane over them. When you put on your play you should make growling noises for your audience.

Use a stick to hold up your shadow puppet. Tape the stick firmly to the back of the puppet so it doesn't move. Be sure not to let your own shadow show up on the screen.

● Shadows with hands

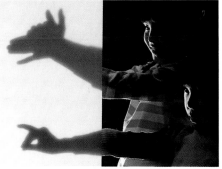

▲ Can you make shadows like these?

● Shadows with dolls

▲ Dolls also make good shadow puppets.

? Can You Make a Vegetable Stamp?

ANSWER If you cut open a green pepper or a lemon you will see that it has a very different shape on the inside than on the outside. If you put paint on the cut end you can use it as a stamp to make a picture on a piece of paper. If you stamp the paper many times you can create a design. Try using another object such as a leaf. You can put paint on a vegetable like a carrot or potato and roll it across the paper.

■ **Materials**

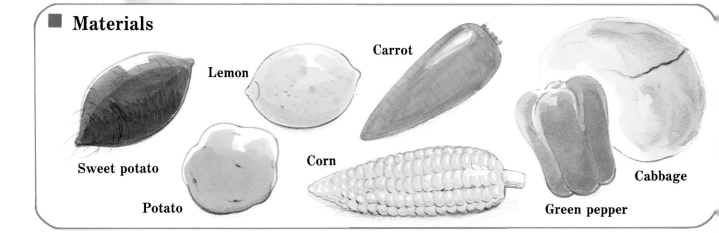

Sweet potato

Lemon

Carrot

Potato

Corn

Green pepper

Cabbage

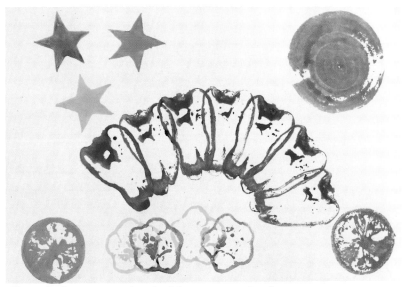

These designs were printed with stamps made of potato, green pepper, lemon and onion. Try making some of your own designs with vegetables.

TRY THIS

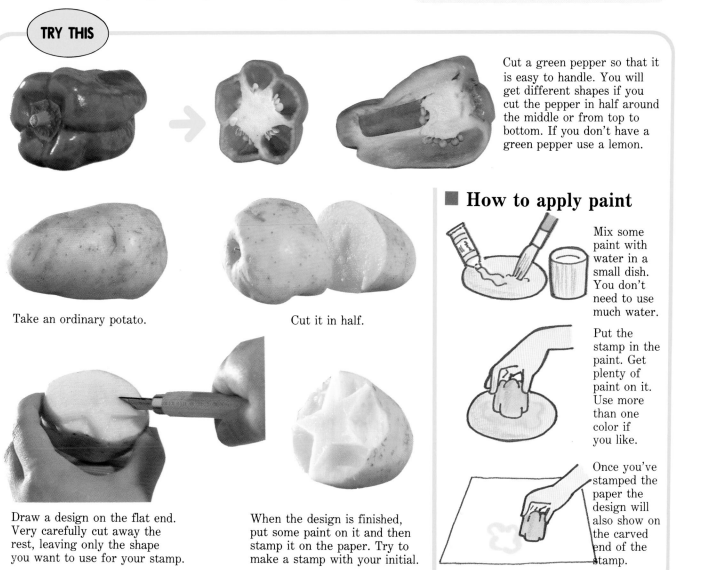

Cut a green pepper so that it is easy to handle. You will get different shapes if you cut the pepper in half around the middle or from top to bottom. If you don't have a green pepper use a lemon.

Take an ordinary potato.

Cut it in half.

Draw a design on the flat end. Very carefully cut away the rest, leaving only the shape you want to use for your stamp.

When the design is finished, put some paint on it and then stamp it on the paper. Try to make a stamp with your initial.

■ How to apply paint

Mix some paint with water in a small dish. You don't need to use much water.

Put the stamp in the paint. Get plenty of paint on it. Use more than one color if you like.

Once you've stamped the paper the design will also show on the carved end of the stamp.

17

Do You Know How to Make a Jigsaw Puzzle?

ANSWER Jigsaw puzzles are pictures that are constructed by fitting many separate little pieces together. Sometimes one piece will have a whole picture in it or maybe just part of a picture. You can make a jigsaw puzzle using a picture or a photograph from a magazine.

Start from the outside and you can finish more quickly.

■ Materials

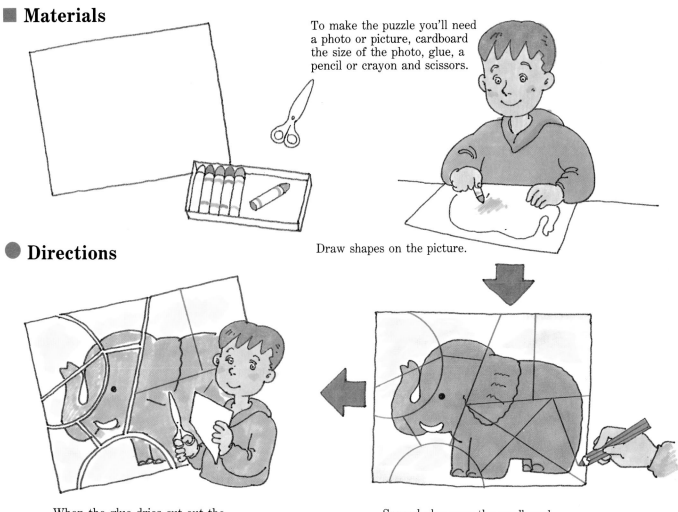

To make the puzzle you'll need a photo or picture, cardboard the size of the photo, glue, a pencil or crayon and scissors.

Draw shapes on the picture.

● Directions

When the glue dries cut out the shapes using your scissors. Your jigsaw puzzle is now complete.

Spread glue over the cardboard. Carefully glue the picture to the cardboard. Be sure to smooth it out so that there aren't any wrinkles.

TRY THIS

Why not try writing a message for your friend and then turning it into a jigsaw puzzle? Put the pieces in an envelope and send it to a friend. Think of how much fun he'll have trying to solve the puzzle and reading your message.

What Kinds of Things Can You Make With Rocks?

ANSWER The next time you visit a riverside or seashore collect some unusual rocks and take them home. With a little imagination you can use them to make some funny animals. All it takes is some materials you can find around the house such as paint, glue, paper and ribbons. How many different animals can you make?

■ Materials

Try making your own toy animals by using all kinds of everyday things like rocks, a felt-tipped pen, modeling clay, yarn, glue, lace, colored construction paper, pipe cleaners and paints. Imagine a zoo filled with the animals you've made.

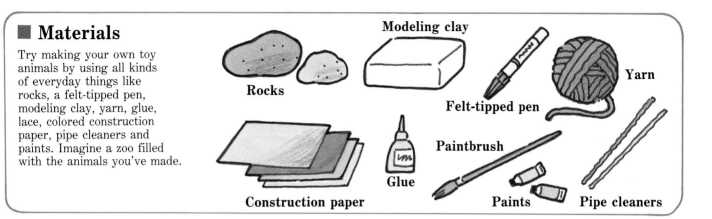

Modeling clay

Rocks

Felt-tipped pen

Yarn

Construction paper

Glue

Paintbrush

Paints

Pipe cleaners

■ What can you make with rocks?

A dog
Find a rock that looks like a dog's head. Attach ears and eyes made out of modeling clay. Should your dog have pointed ears or do you like big floppy ones?

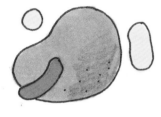

Use a felt-tipped pen to draw in the eyes. Don't forget that dogs have big wet noses. You can draw a mouth too.

A rooster
Find a rock that looks like a bird. Make the rooster's comb and beak out of colored construction paper. Glue them in place to make the head.

Glue on paper eyes and then draw in the pupils using a felt-tipped pen or paint them on with your paintbrush.

Make legs out of pipe cleaners or toothpicks and glue these on next.

Other ideas
Here is an idea of what you can do with more than one rock. For these you have to use a good strong glue. Try to think of some other kinds of animals you can make.

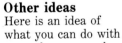

What Animals Can You Make Out of Vegetables?

ANSWER You can use almost any fruit or vegetable to make an animal or doll. You can even combine parts of two different vegetables or fruits. Toothpicks or small sticks can be used to hold all the pieces together and to make legs and necks.

Remember to be careful when you use a knife or any other sharp object.

A penguin. Make the head and body from a cucumber. Attach celery to the body using toothpicks, and make eyes with map pins.

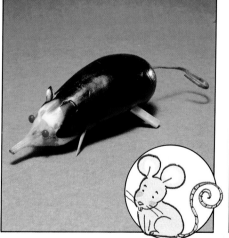

A mouse. Use eggplant slices for the ears and stand them up. Use sticks for the legs and a piece of wire for the tail. Use map pins for eyes.

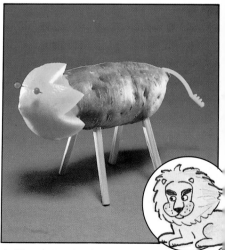

A lion. Use half a lemon for the head. Trim the edge to look like a mane. Use a sweet potato for the body. String makes a good tail.

■ Materials

Sticks

Map pins

Toothpicks

Knife

Vegetables

● Directions

When you need to support a head that's heavy, use a sturdy stick. It's a good idea to sharpen the stick first. Be careful not to split the body with it.

Be sure that your animal can balance on its legs. For light animals try pipe cleaners.

Use toothpicks to connect the small parts. Sometimes you need more than one toothpick. Flatten the edges of round parts to hide the toothpicks.

Use pins to tack on eyes and ears, arms and wings, and even feathers.

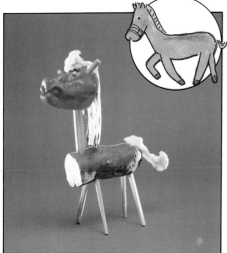

A horse. Use a green pepper for the head, cauliflower for the mane and tail, and sticks for the neck and legs. A sweet potato makes the body.

A spider. Attach legs made of pipe cleaners to a peanut and then use two pins to make the eyes. Do you know how many legs a spider has?

❓ What Can You Make Out of Clay?

ANSWER You can make both animal and human figures with clay. Since a body is made up of many parts, first learn the right order for putting a figure together. Try to construct an animal that looks like it's the real thing.

> If you begin with a frame of strong wire or sticks, the results will look more realistic.

Dog made of modeling clay ▲

Take your time and do a good job

Use four lumps of clay to make the legs. Use a big lump for the body. Add the legs. Support the neck with a stick.

Begin with plenty of clay to build your figure. Outline the shape with a dull putty knife. Then carve out the shape you want.

When making long parts use a stick to support them.

Sheep made of modeling clay ▲

Hippopotamus made of modeling clay ▲

Make Your Own Clay

■ Materials

1½ cups flour   ½ cup salt   ¼ cup vegetable oil   ½ cup water   Bowl   Spoon

● Directions

Mix flour and salt well in the bowl.

Add water and vegetable oil a little at a time while mixing.

Knead the mixture three or four minutes, until it becomes clay. If it cracks it is too dry. Add water by wetting your hands.

Keep your homemade clay in an airtight container or vinyl bag and store it in the refrigerator. If the clay becomes too sticky just add a little more flour.

● To the Parent

Modeling clay is one of the most valuable educational materials children of all ages can play with. As they mature they are able to attempt increasingly more difficult techniques. Small children are content to work with clay using only their hands and primarily are concerned only with the general shape of things. As they grow older and learn to use such tools as a putty knife they can create more detailed forms. Older children can begin projects by first building a wire frame over which a figure can be sculpted using a clay mound on a baseboard. In addition to the recreational benefits of working with clay, children acquire an understanding of the shape of human and animal bodies.

How Do You Make Candles With Different Shapes?

ANSWER Candles are made out of a wax called paraffin. Paraffin wax melts when it is heated and hardens when it cools. Because it goes easily from a liquid to a solid, paraffin is good for molding into candles. You can makes candles of your own with items found around the house. When doing this be sure to ask an adult to help you. Hot wax can easily burn your skin so you have to be very careful. And don't forget to protect your work area with newspaper or a large piece of cardboard.

You must ask a grown-up to help you make candles.

■ Materials

Paraffin Mold Can Cup Oil

Crayons Knife Ice Pot

Stick

String Pan Cardboard

● Directions

Place the paraffin and some crayon shavings in the enamel cup. Set the cup in a pot of water and heat it on the stove.

Soak the string in paraffin, then tie it to the stick. Let the string hang straight down into the center of the mold.

Swiss-cheese candle. Pack crushed ice cubes into a container. Pour in the melted paraffin. The ice will melt, leaving a candle that has holes in it.

Striped candle. Using crayon shavings make different-colored batches of melted paraffin. Then pour one color into the mold at a time.

Pour the melted paraffin into the mold. After it has hardened heat the mold a little. Then you can slide the candle out.

Star candle. Spread oil in a cake pan. Pour in melted paraffin. When it starts to harden, cut out two stars.

Place a string between the two pieces, like a sandwich.

How Do You Make Paper Airplanes?

ANSWER There are many different kinds of paper airplanes. Some are made simply by folding paper. Others must be cut and folded. Some paper airplanes fly a long way in a straight direction. Others will fly in circles and loops.

Look at these unusual paper airplanes

How Can I Make One?

● The squid plane

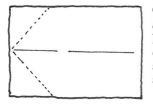

Take a rectangular piece of paper and fold it in half lengthwise. Take two corners at the same end and fold them in so they almost touch the center.

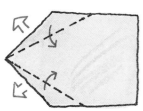

Turn the paper over and fold the same two corners again but this time in the opposite way. Fold them so that they meet right on the center line.

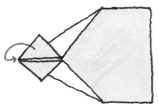

Lift the front tips from underneath the front of the plane, so that two small triangles are formed as shown here.

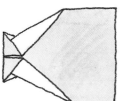

Fold the pointed front tip under. When you've done this, the plane should have a flat front end or leading edge.

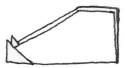

Fold the sheet in half along the center line.

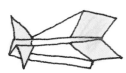

Fold the wings down on each side about one third up from the center line. Then fold the front tips downward as shown here.

● The swallow plane

Take a sheet of paper and begin by folding it over three ways to make creases on the dotted lines shown here, and fold the end over.

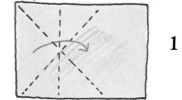 **1**

Fold two smaller triangular flaps out from the center. Their tips should meet at the front end of the plane.

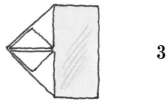 **3**

Fold the entire sheet in half along the dotted line.

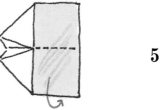 **5**

Use scissors to cut curved sections out of the wings. Be sure they're the same.

Fold along the creases again so that you make two sets of triangles tucked under a large triangle.

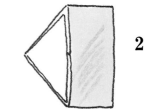 **2**

Fold the end point backwards so that the front of the plane now has a flat, blunt end as you can see here.

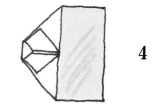 **4**

Close-up of the front end. Notice how it's folded back.

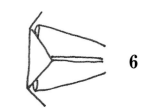 **6**

Hold the plane by the front end and throw it overhand.

7

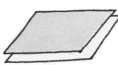

A carefully built plane flies best

If the fold is too wide, use a paper clip.

For strength try using two sheets of paper.

Add flaps to the wings for a more stable flight.

How Do You Make Finger Puppets Out of Peanuts?

ANSWER Find a large peanut and carefully cut the shell in half, taking care not to crush it. Remove the nuts, and then draw faces on the shell halves. If you want, add a little hair or a hat. You have a puppet that fits right on your fingertip.

Paper finger puppets

Make Peanut Puppets

Directions

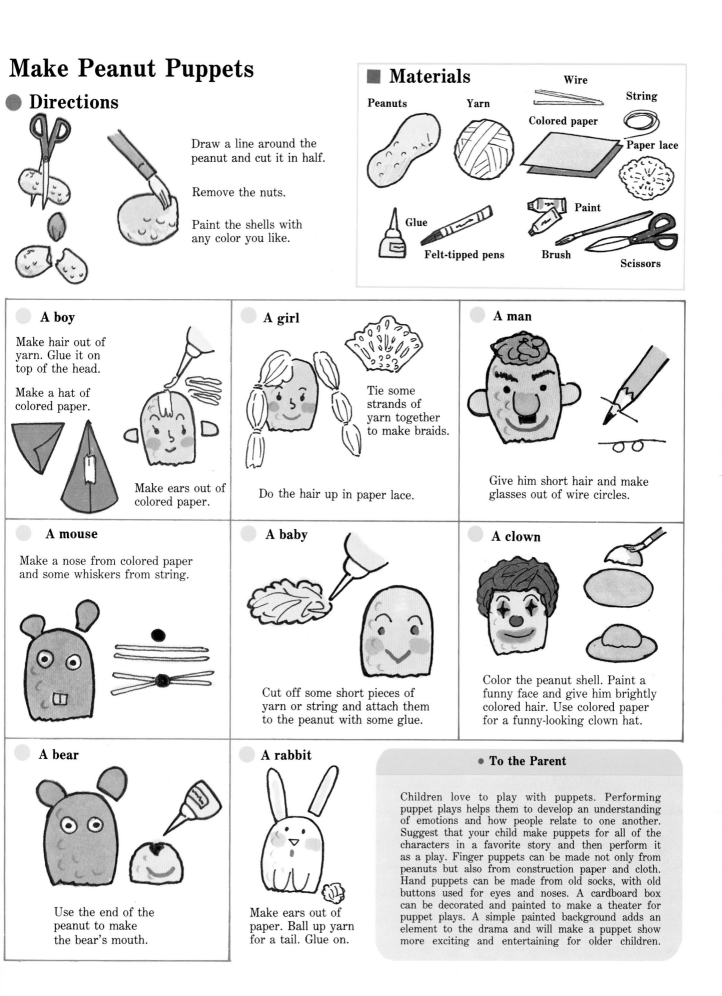

Draw a line around the peanut and cut it in half.

Remove the nuts.

Paint the shells with any color you like.

■ Materials

Peanuts Yarn Wire String Colored paper Paper lace Glue Felt-tipped pens Paint Brush Scissors

A boy

Make hair out of yarn. Glue it on top of the head.

Make a hat of colored paper.

Make ears out of colored paper.

A girl

Tie some strands of yarn together to make braids.

Do the hair up in paper lace.

A man

Give him short hair and make glasses out of wire circles.

A mouse

Make a nose from colored paper and some whiskers from string.

A baby

Cut off some short pieces of yarn or string and attach them to the peanut with some glue.

A clown

Color the peanut shell. Paint a funny face and give him brightly colored hair. Use colored paper for a funny-looking clown hat.

A bear

Use the end of the peanut to make the bear's mouth.

A rabbit

Make ears out of paper. Ball up yarn for a tail. Glue on.

● To the Parent

Children love to play with puppets. Performing puppet plays helps them to develop an understanding of emotions and how people relate to one another. Suggest that your child make puppets for all of the characters in a favorite story and then perform it as a play. Finger puppets can be made not only from peanuts but also from construction paper and cloth. Hand puppets can be made from old socks, with old buttons used for eyes and noses. A cardboard box can be decorated and painted to make a theater for puppet plays. A simple painted background adds an element to the drama and will make a puppet show more exciting and entertaining for older children.

How Do You Go About Making a Mobile?

ANSWER A mobile is a decoration that's made of several pieces hanging in perfect balance. The parts of the mobile should swing easily in the slightest breeze. It's easy to design and put together a mobile that you can enjoy having as a decoration in your room.

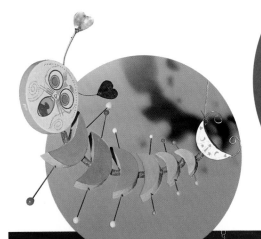

How to Make a Mobile Out of Seashells

■ **Materials**

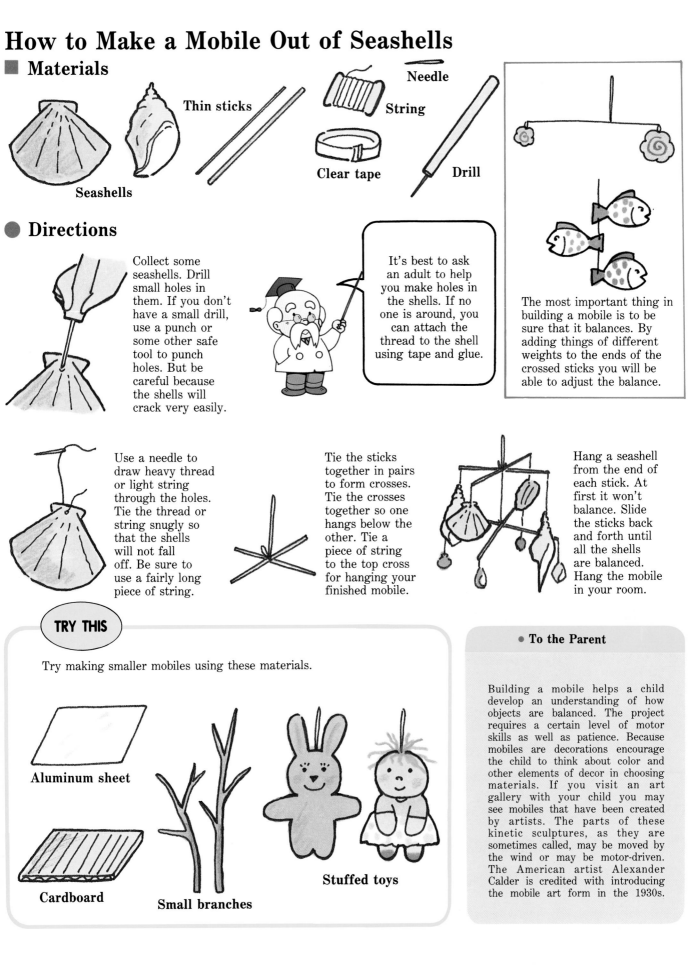

Thin sticks

Needle

String

Clear tape

Drill

Seashells

● **Directions**

Collect some seashells. Drill small holes in them. If you don't have a small drill, use a punch or some other safe tool to punch holes. But be careful because the shells will crack very easily.

It's best to ask an adult to help you make holes in the shells. If no one is around, you can attach the thread to the shell using tape and glue.

The most important thing in building a mobile is to be sure that it balances. By adding things of different weights to the ends of the crossed sticks you will be able to adjust the balance.

Use a needle to draw heavy thread or light string through the holes. Tie the thread or string snugly so that the shells will not fall off. Be sure to use a fairly long piece of string.

Tie the sticks together in pairs to form crosses. Tie the crosses together so one hangs below the other. Tie a piece of string to the top cross for hanging your finished mobile.

Hang a seashell from the end of each stick. At first it won't balance. Slide the sticks back and forth until all the shells are balanced. Hang the mobile in your room.

TRY THIS

Try making smaller mobiles using these materials.

Aluminum sheet

Cardboard

Small branches

Stuffed toys

● **To the Parent**

Building a mobile helps a child develop an understanding of how objects are balanced. The project requires a certain level of motor skills as well as patience. Because mobiles are decorations encourage the child to think about color and other elements of decor in choosing materials. If you visit an art gallery with your child you may see mobiles that have been created by artists. The parts of these kinetic sculptures, as they are sometimes called, may be moved by the wind or may be motor-driven. The American artist Alexander Calder is credited with introducing the mobile art form in the 1930s.

Why Does a Boomerang Return to the Thrower?

(ANSWER) Boomerangs were invented by the native people of Australia, who used them as weapons. They threw them with deadly accuracy at the animals they were hunting. Boomerangs, which are designed to return to the thrower, are also used for sport now.

▲ **An Australian boomerang**

3

It climbs to point 3 and then dives to point 4.

4

A spinning boomerang first flies in the direction you have thrown it.

1

Hold the boomerang by one end with the other end pointed up. Throw it with a twist to send it spinning.

It changes direction again at point 4 and begins to slow down, rotating as it falls toward the ground.

■ Boomerangs and saucers

▼ Toy boomerang

This is the traditional shape of a flying boomerang.

▲ Y-shaped boomerang

The angle of the three wings is very important.

▲ Flying saucer

Throwing a disk back and forth with friends can be a lot of good fun.

▲ Flying saucer

If you throw it up, out and away from yourself, it will return to you.

▲ Cross boomerang

Throw it like a traditional boomerang or horizontally, the way you would a saucer.

If the boomerang does not strike anything at point 2, it will turn away toward the left.

2

■ The boomerang's shape

A boomerang's arms are like the wings on an airplane. They are curved on the top and flat on the bottom. When you throw a boomerang air moves over the curved side a little faster. The air below lifts the boomerang into the air. Because of its shape the forces on a spinning boomerang are not the same at all places. That's why it curves as it flies through the air.

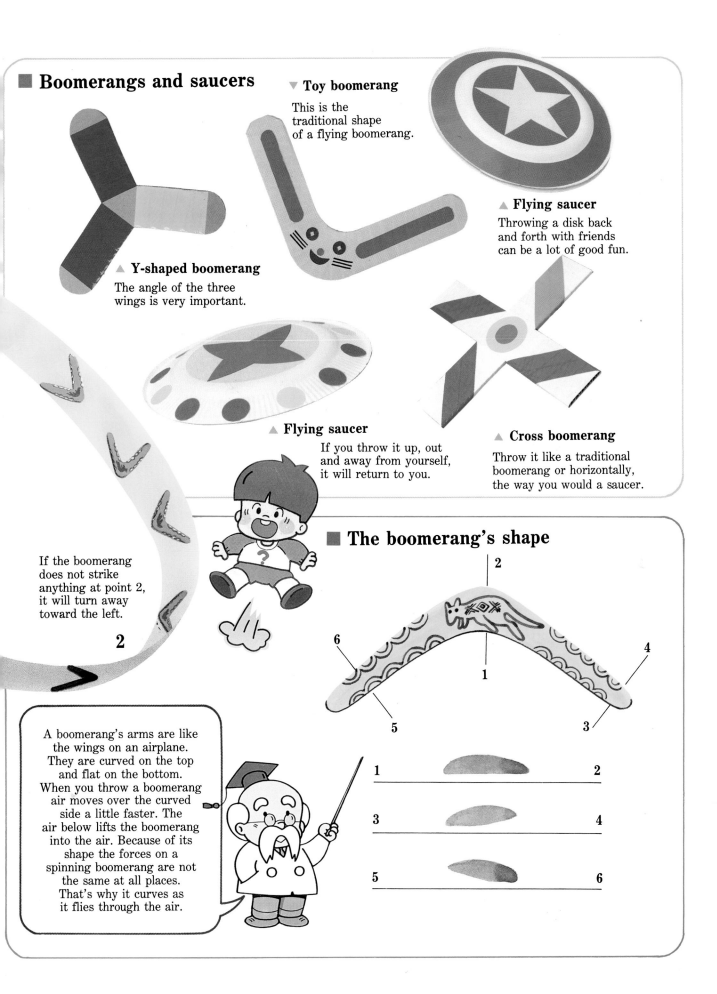

35

How Do You Build a Kite?

ANSWER A kite needs a light, strong framework made of sticks. The framework is covered with a thin material such as paper or cloth. There are many kinds of kites found throughout the world. Kites are very often painted with pictures of faces, birds and other fancy designs.

▲ Brazilian kite

▼ German kite

▲ European kite

◀ American kite

Japanese kite ▲

36

How to Build a Kite

● A floppy kite

Materials

Sticks

Kite string

Plastic bag

Clear tape

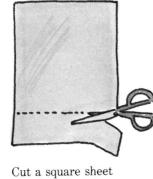

Cut a square sheet out of a plastic bag. Make a large round hole in the center.

Make a cross with sticks and tie them together with kite string. Use clear tape to attach the plastic firmly to the frame.

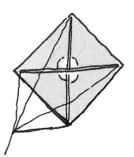

Take four strings the same length. Tie one to each corner, then tie them all to a long kite string.

● A paper bag kite

Materials

Paper bag

Cardboard

String

Glue

Felt-tipped pen

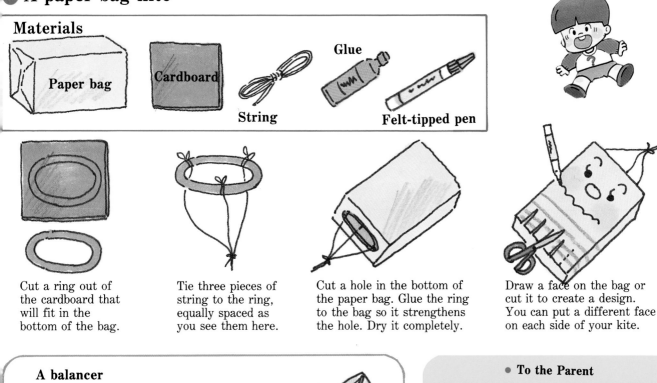

Cut a ring out of the cardboard that will fit in the bottom of the bag.

Tie three pieces of string to the ring, equally spaced as you see them here.

Cut a hole in the bottom of the paper bag. Glue the ring to the bag so it strengthens the hole. Dry it completely.

Draw a face on the bag or cut it to create a design. You can put a different face on each side of your kite.

A balancer

If you attach streamers or a tail to your kite it will fly better.

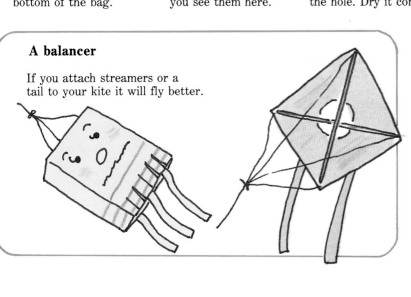

Do You Know How To Build a Model Volcano?

ANSWER Volcanoes exist in many parts of the world. Most are not active. When a volcano is active large white clouds of steam and ash rise into the sky. Red-hot liquid rock, called lava, flows out too. You can build a model volcano with vinegar and baking soda. Make-believe lava will pour out its top even though there is no fire. You can build a realistic volcanic cone out of clay.

◀ Lava streams out of a volcano.

◀ A volcano erupting

Making a Volcano

■ Materials

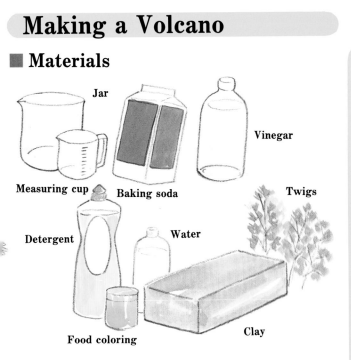

Jar

Vinegar

Measuring cup Baking soda Twigs

Detergent Water

Food coloring Clay

First build a model volcano out of clay. If you don't want to use clay you can just pile up mud or dirt to make it look like a real volcano. But be sure to leave room at the top for the jar to fit in. When your model is ready, put three or four small spoonfuls of baking soda in the jar. Mix together one half cup of water, one fourth of a cup of detergent, a fourth of a cup of vinegar and some red food coloring. Pour the mixture into the jar. Smoke and the lava you've made will start pouring out the way they come from a real volcano.

Add twigs at the bottom.

You can put in the baking soda before building the volcano.

TRY THIS

Volcanoes sometimes erupt in the ocean. Here's how to make an underwater volcano.

To do it you will need a large glass jar, a small bottle, string and red food coloring.

Fill the jar with cold water.

Fill the small bottle with hot water. Tie a string around it and add some red food coloring.

Holding one end of the string, lower the small bottle carefully into the glass jar and watch as "lava" rises from the small bottle. You've just made a mini-volcano.

● To the Parent

Mixing baking soda and vinegar produces the gas carbon dioxide. This reaction yields many tiny bubbles. It is the same kind of reaction that creates the air pockets found in certain breads that are made without yeast. Children can add red food coloring to baking soda and vinegar to create a make-believe volcanic eruption. Adding detergent increases the bubbles, but be sure to check the label. Some detergents produce toxic gases when mixed with other substances. Remind your child to make his or her volcano in a place that's easy to clean.

? How Do You Make An Hourglass?

ANSWER Before there were clocks people used hourglasses to tell time. An hourglass measures time by the speed at which sand falls through a tiny opening. You can make an hourglass using just sand and some other things that are easy to find. You can decide how much sand to use and how fast it should fall.

The difficult thing is to make the sand flow evenly. It's a good idea to experiment before you put it together.

■ Materials

Two glass jars

Cardboard

Clear tape

Glue

Hole puncher

Sand or dry salt

● Directions

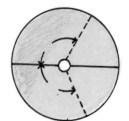

Carefully cut two disks out of cardboard. Make a tiny hole in the center of each disk. Cut sections out of the disks as shown here.

Roll the remaining cardboard sections into cones so that they just fit inside the two glass jars and then tape them.

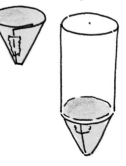

■ Make a water clock

Glue flat lids of two glass jars together so that they fit tightly and let the glue dry. Punch two holes in them large enough for a drinking straw to pass through. Put straws in the holes and seal the holes with putty so water cannot leak through. Let it dry. Fill one of the jars with colored water. That will make it easy to see the water. Then screw the jars onto the lids. Turn them so that the water jar is on top. If the straws are thin it will take longer for the water to drip through. When you know how long it takes for the water to go through you can use your clock for timing different things.

Glue the lids of the two jars together. When they dry ask an adult to punch a hole in each top. If you wish, first test the size of the hole to see how quickly the sand flows. The sand should not flow too fast. If you are using salt be sure to keep it very dry so it will not plug up the holes.

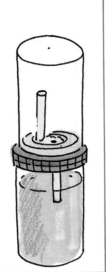

Glue the cones to the jar lids so that their narrow ends surround the holes you've put in the tops. Be sure that you don't bend the wide ends or the sand will leak around the edge.

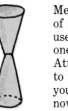

Measure the amount of sand you want to use and put it in one of the jars. Attach the jars to the caps and your hourglass is now ready for use.

❓ How Do You Make Decorations For a Party?

ANSWER You can decorate a table or an entire room. Keep in mind the kind of party and the number of guests. If you make snacks they should be decorative too. They will make your party even better.

▲ Napkin and straw holders are made of paper cups.

▲ Make place mats and fork rests of cardboard or paper.

◄ Decorate grapefruit halves with sails.

▶ Cut a pineapple in half and decorate it with candy.

Make Hanging Decorations

● Some ideas

Fold a square sheet of paper as shown here. Use thin paper. It is much easier to fold and cut.

Cut slits in the folded paper as shown. You can also cut small circular or triangular holes.

Carefully unfold the paper. You'll have a beautiful lace pattern like a snowflake.

■ Materials

Cardboard shapes
Clear tape
Thin paper
Glue
Paint
String
Paintbrush

Place strings inside the cardboard and attach the two halves with clear tape.

Tear thin paper into small pieces and glue them to the cardboard.

Paint pictures on the paper. You can use designs or draw faces.

Decorate a table

● Candy necklace

Tape wrapped candies together in a chain to make a necklace.

● Popcorn holder

Fold a large square sheet of paper as shown here. Fold the bottom up and tape it closed.

Put in a cup. Tie it with a pretty ribbon.

Decorate the outside, then fill it up.

▲ A watermelon cat

Hollow out a watermelon, fill it with fruit and add decoration.

● **To the Parent**

Everyone loves a party, and there are so many occasions to hold one, such as birthdays, holidays and graduations. Encourage your children to participate in the planning for a party. Let them help make the decorations and decide who the guests will be. Preparing and delivering invitation cards is also a good practice. This way a child learns the importance of social skills and can take responsibility as an active member of the family.

❓ What Can You Do With String?

ANSWER String is such a useful material. It's perfect for tying packages and keeping things in bundles. You can also use string to play a lot of different games. You can make up designs by connecting lengths of string to pegs. You can make dolls out of string. You can even make ropeways. With a friend you can play cat's cradle using a loop of string. You can also knit or sew and do other kinds of crafts with string.

String patterns

Push nails into the ground. Connect them with string to make pretty patterns. Or put push pins in a bulletin board. Then you can hang a string picture on the wall.

How to make a string doll

Body

Loop the string and tie it as you see it here.

Head

Wrap the extra string into a ball to make a head.

Cut the loop to make legs.

Hair

Make hair this way and glue it on.

Make clothes by tying string on at the neck and at the waist.

A rabbit ropeway

Make a cutout rabbit from a piece of cardboard and poke a hole in the center of it. Pull a long piece of string through the hole and attach one end to a tree. Lift or lower it to move the rabbit.

How to play cat's cradle

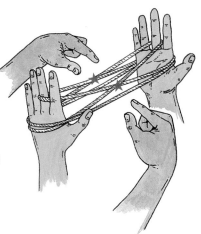

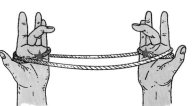

1 Start with loop of string around hands, except thumbs. Twist each hand under to pick up loop. Put middle fingers under opposite loop from below and pull apart.

2 Second player: Take hold of each X with thumbs and forefingers. Pull them up, out and under the side strings, then up through the middle. Pull hands apart.

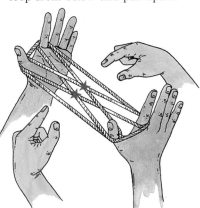

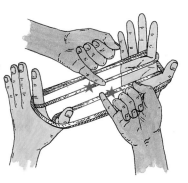

3 First player: With thumbs and forefingers, take hold of long Xs from above, pull them up and over outside strings, then up through middle. Pull hands apart.

4 Second player: Cross over the little fingers and pick up inside strings from opposite sides. Pull them back across each other and over outer strings.

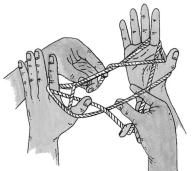

5 Now, holding strings in little fingers by crooking them, put thumbs and forefingers under outer strings and up middle. Pick up both strings as you go.

6 Hold all strings carefully. Pull them apart. This is called the manger. The game can continue, picking up strings from above or below in a similar manner.

What Can You Make With Cloth?

ANSWER There are lots of things you can make with cloth. The easiest kinds of cloth to work with are cotton and felt. Cotton is very light. Felt is thick and heavy. The kind of cloth you choose depends on what you want to make. But first you have to learn to thread a needle. That takes practice. You also have to decide what you want to make. Here are some suggestions. Can you come up with some other ideas?

Tissue holder

Mat

Doll

Making a small purse

■ **Materials**

Lining

Cloth

Appliqués

Velcro™

Needle

Thread

Glue

● **Directions**

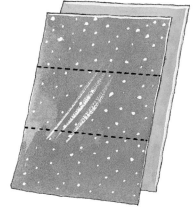

Cut a rectangular piece of cloth and a matching piece of lining.

Fold one third of the cloth over and neatly sew the edges together.

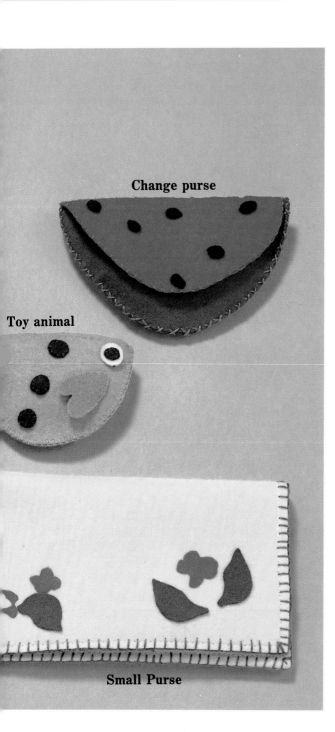

Change purse

Toy animal

Small Purse

■ What cloth is easiest to use?

● **Easy**

Cotton and felt are both easy to use. They have a tight weave that will not loosen up once they have been sewn.

● **Not so easy**

Thick materials do not hold stitches very well. Thin materials like lace and some linings are a real challenge.

■ How to sew

Place the Velcro tape in the positions shown here, and have someone iron it on for you. Glue on appliqués for decoration.

You can buy appliqués in a store, but it's much more fun to make your own. Try to design your own pattern of a flower.

Needlepoint

Sew back and forth from side to side.

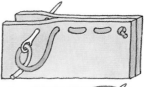

Darning

Put the needle through the cloth. Then go back through the loop.

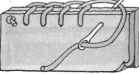

Back stitch

Make one stitch. Go back a half stitch and stitch it again.

47

Can You Do Any Magic Tricks?

ANSWER Have you ever seen a magician performing tricks? Did she pull a rabbit out of a hat or a flower out of a handkerchief? Did she make a woman float in the air? Magicians always claim there is no trick in what they do, but there definitely is. Some tricks are so easy that you can perform them with things you find around the house. Try learning these tricks and amazing your friends.

■ Poking a balloon

Blow up a balloon and hold a needle where people can see it.

Ordinarily if you stick the balloon with the needle it will pop. Ask someone in your audience to demonstrate that the needle will pop a balloon.

Take out a new balloon. Blow it up. While saying "abracadabra," carefully stick a piece of clear tape on the back of it. Be sure that no one sees what you are doing. Then take a needle and poke the balloon where the tape is. Surprise! It won't pop! It looks like magic to those who are watching you do the trick.

■ Vanishing money

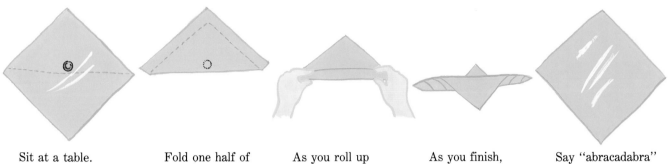

Sit at a table. Now lay out a handkerchief and coin as above.

Fold one half of the handkerchief over the other to hide the coin.

As you roll up the handkerchief let the coin slide forward.

As you finish, the hidden coin will fall into your lap.

Say "abracadabra" and quickly lift the handkerchief. The coin is gone!

■ Magic fingers

Make a loop of brightly colored string and very carefully wrap it around all your fingers.

Reach under the front string and pull the string out from behind thumb and forefinger. Twist the loop.

Act mysterious and put this loop of string over your forefinger and do the same to the other fingers.

After putting loops of string over all your fingers hold them up to show everyone that there is no trick.

Bend your thumb in and pull the front string from the other end. Like magic the knots will disappear!

■ Science magic

You can even use science to perform magic tricks. For this trick you'll need a comb made of hard plastic, a piece of wool and a water faucet.

Turn on a steady stream of water from the faucet. Hold the comb near it. Nothing happens.

Now watch this!

Now take the wool cloth and rub it over the comb. While you are doing this say the famous magic word.

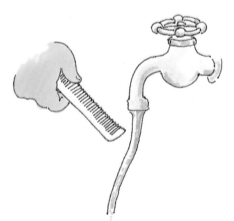

Hold the comb near the flowing water again. This time the water curves toward the comb. When you rub the comb with wool it creates static electricity. This causes the comb to act like a magnet, and it attracts the stream of water.

Can You Write Secret Messages?

ANSWER If vinegar or the juice of some fruits and vegetables dries on paper it leaves no stain. But if the paper is then heated a stain will show. Try making ink out of one of these liquids. When the ink dries the letters will disappear. Only someone who knows the secret will be able to read your invisible letter.

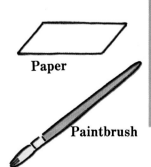

It's almost like writing with a secret code.

1 Here's a letter. Can you read it?

2 Gee, I can't tell what it is. I don't see anything there.

How do you do it?

■ **Materials**

Lemon

Dish

Paper

Paintbrush

● **Directions**

Put some lemon juice in a dish. Dip a paint brush in the lemon juice. Draw a picture.

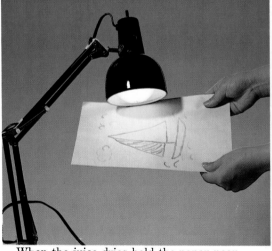

When the juice dries hold the paper near a hot light bulb to bring out the picture.

3

I know! It's invisible ink! It will show up if I heat it carefully.

4

I found you! Thanks a lot for sending me that secret map!

MINI-DATA

You can use orange or radish juice or even some thinned vinegar. The dried colors that appear after heating will depend on the juice you use. Try it!

Vinegar

Orange

Radish

What Do You Think It Is?

What is it? Eyes? A mustache? When the paper is heated, pictures of a cat, a bird and a caterpillar will appear.

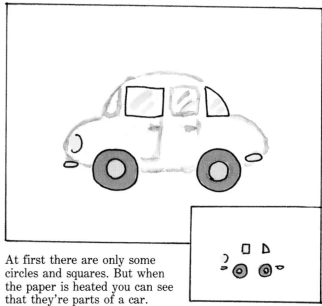

At first there are only some circles and squares. But when the paper is heated you can see that they're parts of a car.

● **To the Parent**

Before microfilm was invented spies sometimes sent messages written in invisible ink. The secret message could be hidden between the lines of a letter or a book. Invisible ink is not nearly sophisticated enough for today's spies, but children can still have fun using it. To prevent accidents be sure to instruct your child in the careful use of a heat source such as a hot plate or light bulb. In addition to sending messages in invisible ink children like to invent their own secret codes for writing those messages. Encourage children to create a new secret code, which can be made up of everyday symbols, numbers or a more elaborate hieroglyphic formula.

? How Do You Make Ice Cream?

ANSWER To make ice cream you mix milk or cream with sugar or honey. Some people like to put in some eggs too. Then you add flavoring. Three of the most popular flavors are chocolate, vanilla and strawberry, but there are lots of other flavors. What's your favorite? You can even add some fresh fruit for flavoring. Once everything is mixed together you freeze it. And when it's done you will have your own ice cream to enjoy just as you like it.

▲ Would you like this for dessert tonight?

■ **Materials**

1 teaspoon gelatin

2 cups milk

½ cup honey

1 teaspoon vanilla

1 cup evaporated milk

Whisk

Large bowl

½ cup nuts

¼ cup warm water

● Directions

Put warm water in bowl, add gelatin and blend it in well.	Add one cup of milk and the honey, and mix.	Add vanilla, the rest of the milk, evaporated milk, and mix.
Put bowl and contents in freezing compartment of your refrigerator.	Leave it in the freezer for two hours or until it is very hard.	Beat the mixture with a whisk to make it soft and frothy.
Mix in the nuts, stirring lightly. You may use fruit if you prefer.	Put it back into the freezer and leave it there another two hours.	Once it has hardened take the ice cream out and serve it up!

Decorate your ice cream treats with chocolate, fruit and other things you like.

Fruit

Bananas

Whipped cream

Strawberries

Grapefruit

Ice cream parfait   **Ice cream sundae**   **Strawberry grapefruit bowl**

❓ What's a Good Way To Invite Birds Into the Yard?

ANSWER The best way to attract birds is to build a bird bath or feeder in a quiet part of the yard where people do not go. Prepare food that birds will like, and be careful not to disturb them when you watch them. You may be able to see many different kinds of birds.

■ Where's a good place?

Build it in the garden or in an empty spot near the house.

A balcony can be a good place if people don't use it often.

Tips for bird watchers

Birds of the same type look very much the same. If you want to tell them apart pay close attention to their beaks and legs. That's where birds are most likely to be different.

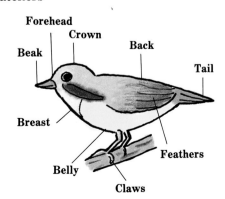

Forehead
Crown
Beak
Back
Tail
Breast
Feathers
Belly
Claws

▲ Most finches love seeds.

▲ These birds like to eat fruit.

Build a Bird Feeder

■ Materials

Wooden box   Post

Hammer

Nails

Stick

Net

String

Nail the box to the top of the post. Use enough nails to be sure it's sturdy.

Place it outside, and scatter seeds and other food in it. Watch for birds.

Fill the net with seeds and other food. Tie the sticks together and then tie the bag of bird feed to the sticks.

Build a bird bath

■ Materials

Tin box

Thick stick

Strong glue

Glue the empty box to the top of the stick. Use a nail if the glue doesn't hold well enough.

What do birds eat?

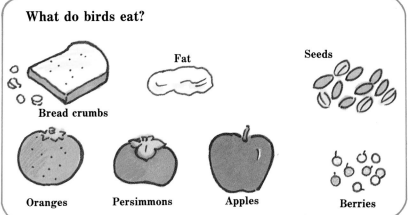

Bread crumbs

Fat

Seeds

Oranges   Persimmons   Apples   Berries

● **To the Parent**

The use of pesticides and the cutting down of forests have seriously threatened many species of birds. Inviting birds to your yard is not only good for your child, it's also good for the birds. You can try changing the type of seeds and other food in the feeder to find out what attracts different species. With a little practice children can learn to identify different species of birds and to keep a simple record of those that they have seen. Be sure that your feeder and birdbath are high enough that the birds will not be in danger from stray cats or other predators.

55

How Do You Make Pressed Flowers?

ANSWER Have you ever seen a flower and wished that its beauty would last forever? It is possible to preserve flowers much longer than you might think. You can do it with any pretty flower or wildflower by pressing it between two sheets of absorbent paper. This removes the moisture from the petals. You can use pressed flowers to decorate all kinds of things.

How to Press Flowers

■ Materials

Newspaper

Board

Brick or book

Blotting paper

Flowers

Clear tape

Put the flower on top of the blotting paper and newspaper.

Put another sheet of blotting paper on top of the flower.

Cover with a newspaper and board, then put bricks or books on top.

Wait a week. Remove the flower and mount it on fancy paper.

● How to dry flowers

Flowers can be dried and preserved with special chemicals called desiccants.

Stand flowers in a lump of putty.

Carefully pour in desiccant.

After a week they should be ready.

● How to preserve beautiful colors

Put flowers and some desiccant in a box.

Put desiccant on the flowers, then press them with a weight.

A quick way to dry flowers is to cover them with wax paper. Ask a parent or grown-up to iron it very carefully.

● To the Parent

When making pressed flowers, the key to success is to dry the flower as quickly as possible. Newspaper, blotting paper and a weight will work well enough, but with older children the use of wax paper and an iron may produce better results. Not only flowers but leaves can be preserved in this way. A good project is to fill a notebook with a variety of pressed flowers and leaves and find out what kinds you have. Put the names in the book to help you remember which is which.

? How Do You Build a Terrarium?

ANSWER A terrarium is like an aquarium but for houseplants instead of fish. It can be of any shape or size from a small bottle to a large glass tank. Once you have made it, it doesn't need much care. Plants are quite hardy. What they need is some sunshine and clean water to keep them alive. However, if you decide to add some small frogs, turtles or snails to your terrarium you will have to take special care of them. Then you will have a miniature nature park or zoo.

Materials

Soil
Small stick
Spool
Paper funnel
Jar
Scissors
Spray
Plants

Pour soil through a paper funnel into a large jar until it is about one fourth full. Pack the soil down well.

Dig the plants out of the pots. Trim the roots and leaves to fit in the jar. Leave as much of the roots as possible.

Plant the largest plants first, and then arrange the smaller ones around them in a neat pattern.

• **To the Parent**

Plants thrive inside terrariums as long as there is the right combination of moisture, light and air. Plants that like humidity and low light are best. Most plants will stay healthy in a peat-based potting mixture laid on top of a drainage layer of charcoal and gravel. If the soil dries out try to moisten it with a spray mist. If there is too much water open the terrarium and let some water evaporate.

Terrarium

Prayer plant

Maidenhair fern

Peperomia

Wax plant

Once the jar is closed there should be just enough moisture inside to form drops of water. If there is too much moisture leave the jar open until the extra water has all evaporated.

Place the spool on the end of the stick and use it to pack down the soil quite firmly.

Spray the arrangement with water from the mister. Wipe all the dirt and water off the inside of the jar. Wait for the leaves to dry. Close the jar.

Why Not Grow Your Own Plants?

ANSWER If you plant hyacinth or daffodil bulbs they will sprout and grow. These flowers grow well when placed in the window sill. But you can also grow vegetables indoors. For example if you put soybeans or spice seeds in water they will sprout. Transplant them into pots and take care of them, and they will grow into healthy plants. Parsley and other plants we eat will also grow well indoors.

● Directions

Soak fresh mustard seeds, dill seeds, sesame seeds, caraway seeds or coriander seeds in water overnight. In the morning lay them on a damp sponge. Keep the sponge moist by keeping it in a shallow dish of water. Place the dish in a bright area but not in direct sunlight. The seeds should sprout in two or three days. If you wish you can transplant them to a pot. They will grow into plants if you take care of them. You could start an indoor garden.

Put an onion in a jar or glass of water so that the bottom of the onion is in the water. In a few days green shoots will appear. As the shoots grow larger the onion bulb will grow smaller. Later you can plant it in a pot with soil.

Put a third of a cup of soybeans in a glass with warm water. Soak the seeds overnight. In the morning drain the beans and rinse them in warm water. Cover the glass with cheesecloth and place it in a warm dark place. Rinse the seeds with warm water each morning and evening. In three days your beans will have grown sprouts. To stop them from growing any more place them in the refrigerator. Sprinkle your fresh sprouts on salad.

If plants get plenty of clean water and sunlight there is no need for fertilizer.

TRY THIS

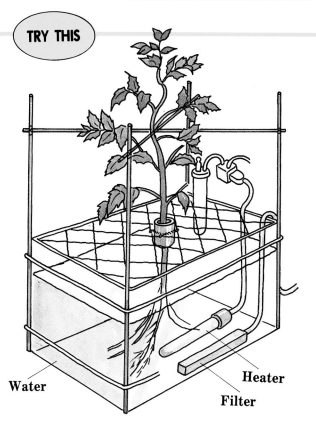

Water

Heater

Filter

Put water containing plant food in a water tank. Keep the water clean and warm, using an aquarium filter and a heater with a thermostat. Place a small cherry tomato plant in the tank and wrap the stem with paper. This will hold it up and prevent the loss of moisture. It may also be necessary to support the base and stalk of the plant with string to keep it from falling. Put it in direct sunlight. The plant should begin flowering in a month. Pollinate the flowers by hand. To do this you should take some pollen grains from the male stamens of the plant and very gently put them on the plant's pistil. You may need to ask an adult to show you these parts of the plant. Keep the water at about 50° to 60°F. (10° to 15°C.). Add plant food weekly. With luck you may eventually grow some cherry tomatoes of your own!

● To the Parent

Hyacinth and tulip bulbs, soybeans, carrots, tomatoes, eggplant and other vegetables can all be easily grown indoors. They'll grow wherever there is plenty of sun, water and fertilizer. Gardening is a good hobby to share with your children. If you use a particular spice when you prepare food you might also try planting it. If your child does decide to grow a cherry tomato plant be sure that the stem is well supported as it grows or it will not be able to support its own weight, and it will break.

❓ How Do You Make Whistles?

ANSWER It's easy to make whistles out of many things you may happen to have around, including paper, leaves, seashells and nuts. The sound will be different depending on what you use. Whistles are one of the oldest kinds of music makers.

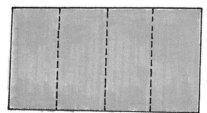

■ Make a paper whistle

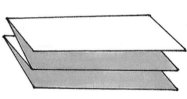

Use a piece of paper about the size and thickness of a postcard. Fold it in half. Then fold each half in the opposite direction.

When it is folded right it will have three pleats like the ones in an accordion.

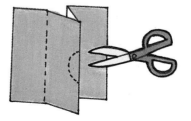

Now poke a hole in the center of the middle crease with a pair of scissors. And don't cut yourself. Hold it to your mouth with the cut side away from you, and blow through this hole.

■ Acorn whistle

Poke or cut a small hole in the top of an acorn and gently remove all the meat, being careful not to make any cracks in the shell.

Blow gently over the top of the hole to make it whistle.

■ Leaf whistle

Find a large, tough leaf. You can easily find these on trees, bushes or on the ground.

Roll it up into a tube from the tip to the stem.

Flatten the end. Put it between your lips. Blow.

■ Seashell whistle

Holes

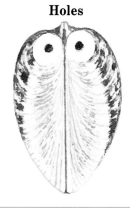

Make two holes in the ends of a clam shell. Be careful, and don't crack the shell.

Blow lightly over the holes to make it whistle.

■ Bamboo flute

Drill out the joints of a stick of bamboo to make it a hollow tube.

Cut a notch in one end and stick a plastic reed in it. Then blow over the reed.

What Do Music Notes Tell Us?

ANSWER Notes show you rhythm by telling you how long a sound should be. They also show you the pitch. Their position on the lines of music tells you how high or low the sounds should be.

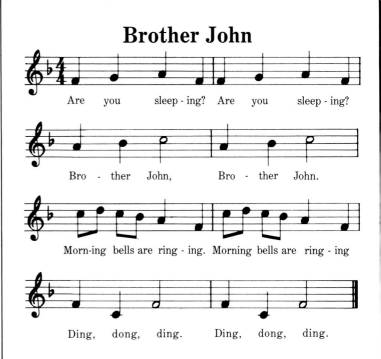

Brother John

Are you sleep - ing? Are you sleep - ing?

Bro - ther John, Bro - ther John.

Morn-ing bells are ring - ing. Morning bells are ring - ing

Ding, dong, ding. Ding, dong, ding.

Notes	Length	Rests	
Whole note		**Whole rest**	A whole note tells you to play or sing the note for four beats or counts of the rhythm. A whole rest tells you that you should not play or sing for four beats.
Half note		**Half rest**	A half note is half as long as a whole note. You play or sing the note for two beats. A half rest is half as long as a whole rest, which means it's two beats long.
Quarter note		**Quarter rest**	A quarter note is so called because it's one fourth the length of a whole note. Play or sing it for one beat. A quarter rest is one beat long.
Eighth note		**Eighth rest**	An eighth note is only one eighth as long as a whole note. It gets only one half of a beat. As you can guess, an eighth rest means you rest for half a beat.

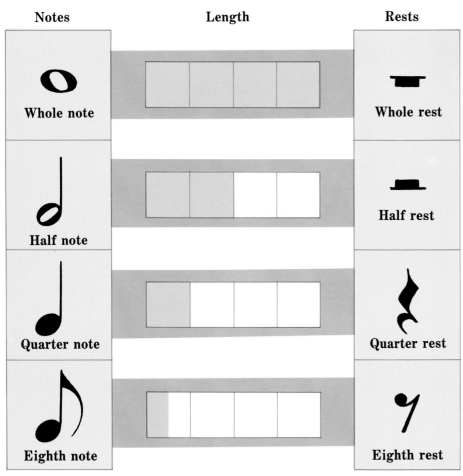

■ Notes and rhythm

Music has a regular beat like the heartbeat you feel in your body. But the beat of music, called rhythm, can combine many kinds of beats at once. There's always a basic beat that you can feel by counting in your head, by tapping your foot or by moving your hands and arms. Along with this basic beat there are other beats that are faster or slower. In music you do many things at once. It may sound difficult, but a little practice is all you need.

Count silently

Tap your foot

Wave your arms

● **To the Parent**

Rhythm is felt instinctively by almost everyone, and children respond naturally to it by moving their body in time with the beat of music. Encourage them to tap their feet or wave their hands to music. Have them clap in time with the sound of music they are familiar with, fitting the words to the rhythm as they sing. In all the counting patterns shown here, a quarter note gets one beat. Marches often use a time signature of 2/2, in which a half note gets one beat. Another common time signature is 6/8, in which an eighth note gets one full beat.

■ **4/4 (four-four) time.** There are four beats in each box, called a measure.

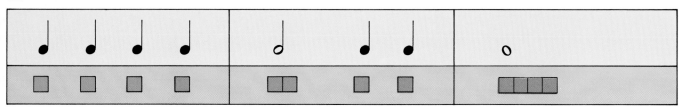

■ **2/4 (two-four) time.** There are two beats in each measure.

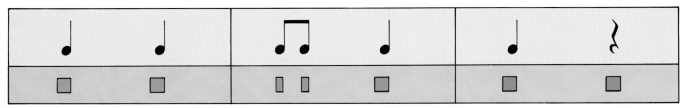

■ **3/4 (three-four) time.** There are three beats in this 3/4 time signature.

TRY THIS

There's rhythm in the way we talk. Practice saying these words, and look at the notes as you say the words. They show that some sounds are long and some are short. Think of some others.

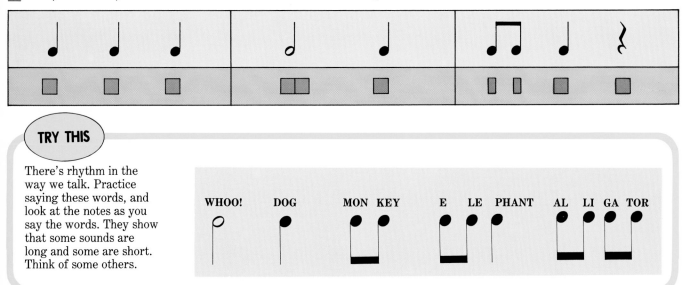

WHOO!　DOG　MON KEY　E LE PHANT　AL LI GA TOR

65

How Do You Play the Piano?

(ANSWER) You make music on a piano by hitting the keys. Each key has a different note. The notes that a piano makes get higher from left to right. Most pianos have 88 keys. The difference between each note is half a tone. Have you ever played a piano? Do you know how to play a scale? Try striking eight white keys in a row.

Try learning how to read music

All music is written in a score. A score is really just directions to playing music. The score tells the tempo of the music, the notes and the length of each note and rest. To play the piano you must first learn to read notes. After that it just takes a lot of practice and hard work.

▼ marks the corresponding notes on the music score and piano.

The G clef is also called the treble clef. It is a symbol to show the position of the note G. When you see this symbol on the staff lines, it shows that the pitch of these notes is high.

The F clef is also called the bass clef. It shows the position of F and also tells us that the pitch of these notes is low.

The ♯ or sharp notation. This tells us that the note will be a half tone higher and to use the next key on the piano keyboard.

The ♭ or flat notation. This means that the note will be a half tone lower and to use the piano key that comes before it.

Natural notation. This symbol is used to show a return up or down the keyboard one half step to the original or natural note.

Why Are the Keys White and Black?

The white keys are used to play the most basic musical scale called C major. Start with a C, as in the drawing on the right. Play only the white keys to the right. You will play a C major scale. All the other scales use the black and white keys. No scale uses only the black keys.

▨ What is a scale?

A scale is the order in which the keys are played in steps from the lowest to the highest tone. There are lots of scales, and each one is played following specific rules. In the illustration the steps are called the major musical scale. Two steps are closer than the rest: between E and F, and B and C. These are half steps, while the wider spacings are called whole steps. The name of a scale is decided by the name of the first note of the scale.

Note: The ♯ and ♭ indicate half steps.

Using both hands together

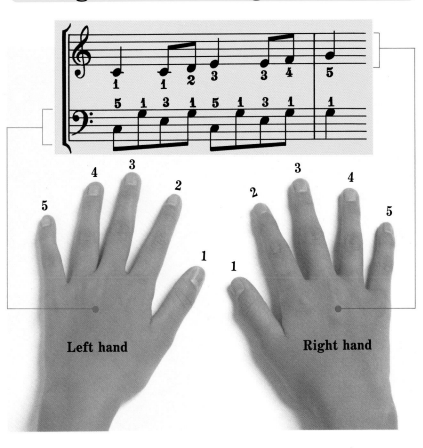

Left hand

Right hand

The right fingers are very important when playing keyboard instruments like the piano, organ and melodeon. Usually it is the right hand that keeps the melody and the left hand that accompanies it. Note that both the right and the left thumbs are numbered 1. Always be sure to follow the numbering in a musical score.

● To the Parent

A young child likes to strike the piano keys and listen to the sounds the different notes make. Soon he or she will be able to play a simple scale. The next step is to show a child what each note looks like when written down. Explain the musical notations to your child while sitting at the piano and show how they work. A book of songs is an excellent way of increasing your child's desire to explore a piano's keyboard. If your child shows continued enthusiasm or natural talent, you may want to consider giving him or her lessons with a professional piano teacher.

? Can You Make Your Own Musical Instruments?

(ANSWER) Many things you find around your house can be used to make musical instruments. Even everyday things like empty bottles and cans, boxes and scraps of wood can be used to make music. If you make several different instruments you can put on a concert for all your friends.

■ Try making these

A box banjo

Cut a hole in a cardboard box and stretch rubber bands over the hole. Use rubber bands of all different sizes.

Maracas

Stick a wooden handle in an empty can. Put some sand or dried beans in it. Cover the holes with tape.

A tambourine

Sew two paper plates together with string. Strike the tambourine with your fingers.

■ Strike up the band!

▲ Marching bands have lots of drums.

When people play musical instruments together it is called a concert. Concerts may be played by very large orchestras and bands led by a conductor or by only a few musicians. In a concert when only one person plays all by himself it is called a solo.

A brass band is formed by bringing together trumpets, trombones, horns, tubas, snare drums, bass drums and some cymbals. Such bands are often used in parades and sporting events. Players in a brass band usually wear colorful hats and fancy uniforms.

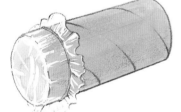

A kazoo
Cover a paper tube with tissue paper and tie it with a rubber band. Hum a tune into the tube to create an interesting sound.

Rhythm blocks
Glue some sandpaper to two wooden blocks and scrape them together to keep rhythm.

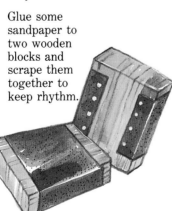

What Can You Do With Empty Cans?

ANSWER There are as many things to do with cans as there are different sizes and shapes of cans. Many of the things you can make don't require much additional material. However it may take you some time to collect enough cans of the same size and shape. Good cans to watch out for are juice and soft drink cans, coffee cans and soup cans. Keep your collection of cans in a place where no one will throw them out.

Coin toss

Bowling

Stilts

Coin toss

Write numbers for points on the bottoms of some empty cans. Join them together with tape or wire. Use coins or stones and toss them into the cans. Keep point totals. The first to score 50 wins.

Kick the can

A runner kicks the can. While the catcher chases it all the runners hide. The catcher must then look for the runners while guarding the can. When a runner is spotted the catcher touches the can and calls his name and location. If a runner kicks the can, all runners hide again.

Stilts

Place two cans of the same size on the ground with the closed ends facing up. Make holes on opposite sides of each can. Run strings through the holes and tie in loops to hold the cans to your feet while you walk on them.

Marionette

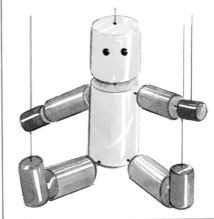

Join a number of different sized cans together with wire in the shape of a doll. Paint on a face and other details. Connect strings to control the arms, legs and head. Can you make your marionette walk? Try dancing.

Can bowling

Set up 10 cans like bowling pins. Knock them down with a ball from about 15 feet (4.5 m) away. You have three tries. You get one point for each can you knock down. The highest score after 10 rounds wins.

Can raft

Plug the holes in some empty juice cans. Join them together as shown using tape and wire. Attach a sail to the raft, set it in the water and watch it float!

Be careful! Never play with cans that have sharp or ragged edges. Always ask an adult to help you punch a hole in a can.

❓ Do You Know How to Play Dodgeball?

(ANSWER) There are many ways of playing dodgeball. With a small group, a few players stand inside a circle. Players outside the circle throw the ball at them. A player who is hit must leave the circle. With a larger number of players, the group forms two teams. They stand on opposite sides of the court and throw the ball at each other.

■ Basic rules

You must leave the court if you are hit by the ball.

If you catch the ball you are safe.

If the ball misses you then it does not count.

■ Other rules

The court should be a rectangle, 25 feet (7.5 m) by 30 feet (9 m), divided in half. Once hit, a player must go to the outside of the other team's end but continues throwing at the other team. The side with the most players after six minutes wins.

▲ If the ball bounces before it hits a player it doesn't count and the player is safe.

▲ Balls thrown while on the boundary line do not count.

◄ A ball caught while on the boundary line goes to the other team.

In circle dodgeball the last person remaining untouched inside the circle is the winner.

● **To the Parent**

Dodgeball is fun and a challenging game for children. Catching and throwing the ball requires good muscle coordination while avoiding being hit means the players must be quick on their feet. The rules and playing area can either be kept simple or made more complicated depending on the ability level of the children. Throwing at the head should always be prohibited to avoid injuries. If possible an adult or older child should supervise to prevent disagreements.

Can You Go Straight In a Forest?

ANSWER It's easy if you pick a destination, then look for landmarks between you and your destination. Follow these landmarks one at a time until you reach your target. If your path is interrupted by a very large landmark climb on top of it or walk around it until you can see your destination clearly again. Large rocks or strangely shaped trees make good landmarks because they are very easy to spot and keep your eyes on.

■ Use a compass

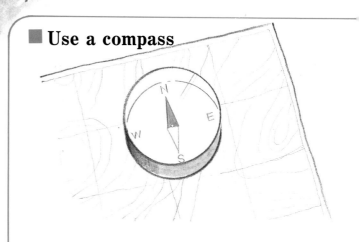

The needle on a compass points north. The top of maps is also north. So turn the map until its top points in the same direction as the needle to orient it with the ground.

How Can We Avoid Getting Lost?

Make trail markers as you go along. Stacks of rocks make good markers. Be sure to put them in places that will be easy to see.

Make arrows out of stones pointing the same way you are traveling. You can also use sticks.

Make trail blazes on tree trunks or branches with bright ribbons or string that will be easy to see.

■ Follow the sun

The sun rises in the east and sets in the west. Check your watch and the sun's position. Knowing east and west you can figure out north and south.

■ Study the stars

Learn to find Polaris, the North Star, in the nighttime sky. This bright star is always in the north. Spot this and you can figure out where you're going.

Here are three ways to find your direction if you get lost.

❓ **What Should You Know Before You Go Camping?**

ANSWER Camping is a chance for friends to live together in a natural setting. Everyone must get along and do a fair share of the chores that are part of camping. When you are living in nature you must pay special attention to changes in the weather, and be careful that you don't get hurt somehow.

▼ A family pitches camp.

Gather wood for fuel. Small pieces are easier to light. If the wood is wet, whittle it into smaller pieces to dry.

Pile up rocks to make a fireplace. Build this out in the open so that the fire will be fanned by the wind.

Dig a drainage ditch around your tent to keep the rain out. And keep clean water handy for washing.

Always take the water from a river upstream from your campsite. River water should always be boiled before you drink it.

■ Tying knots

A square knot

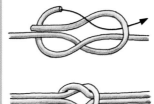

This is a simple knot to tie. But it is not a good knot for large rope or ropes of different sizes. It is often used to join the ends of two cords.

A bowline

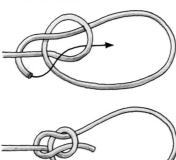

With this knot no matter how hard you pull on the loop it will remain the same size. This is a good knot for tying up a boat or for tying around the body when climbing. Although it is very easy to tie it's very strong.

A timber hitch

This knot is used for fastening ropes to logs or tree trunks. It is very strong.

A half hitch

Wrap the rope around an object, then tie the half hitch. This knot is the basis for many other knots, but it is not very strong.

What Are These Children Doing?

■ Jumping rope

You can jump rope alone or you can have two of your friends hold a long rope and one or more people can jump it at the same time. It can also be a lot of fun to sing songs or play games while jumping rope.

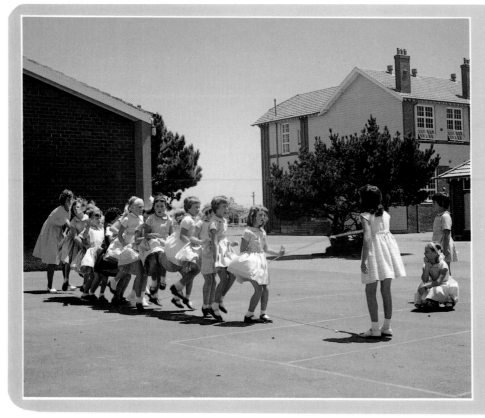

■ Playing cards

A deck of cards has four suits of 13 cards each plus one or two jokers. Suits are spades, hearts, diamonds and clubs. Each has a king, queen and jack, known as face cards, and 10 cards with 1 to 10 spots. The ace has only one spot, but it is the highest card. Hearts and diamonds are red. Spades and clubs are black.

■ Marionettes

A marionette is a puppet controlled by strings. The simple ones have strings for only their head, hands and legs. More complex ones have dozens of individual strings connected to every part of them. In some parts of the world, marionette shows are performed in large theaters. Can you put on a marionette show with some of your friends?

■ Ceramics

Ceramic pots and bowls can be made with the help of a pottery wheel. First the clay is put on the wheel. While the wheel turns, a potter forms the shape with his hands and special tools. Then the shaped clay is baked in an oven to make it hard.

■ Pressing flowers

To press flowers lay them flat inside a large heavy book and close it while they flatten and dry out. A few days later take your pressed flowers out and mount them. Be careful not to damage them.

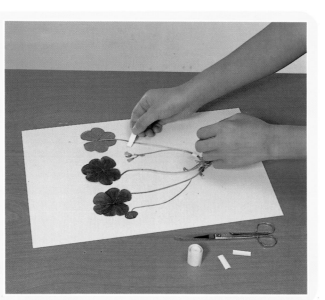

🅀 And What Are These Doing?

■ Embroidering

Sewing pictures with thread is embroidery. Start by gathering lots of different colored threads. Make a design on cloth. Stitch over this design. For a simple project try making a handkerchief.

■ Crocheting

Hats and clothes can be made from a long piece of yarn. There are two methods you can use. One uses a hook and is called crocheting. The other uses two long needles and is known as knitting. In both you can use different stitches or even yarn in different colors. You can make things for yourself or for others.

■ Appliqué

Appliqué is a nice way of decorating fabric. Pieces of colored cloth are sewn to large pieces of fabric in a colorful design. They are attached by many very small stitches around the outside of these pieces of cloth. Because that takes a very long time sometimes people glue these pieces of fabric in place. Some appliqués need only to be ironed onto other cloth.

● To the Parent

Crochet, appliqué and embroidery are old traditions handed down from one generation to another. If you know how to do them pass these interesting hobbies on to your own children.

Growing-Up Album

What Are They Doing?

There are a lot of children playing in a field.
They are doing the things that you have learned to
do. What are they doing? Can you play any of these
games? Would you like to try? Go ahead, pick one.

1. Leaf whistles 2. Paper airplanes
3. Stilts 4. Kite flying 5. Boomerang
6. Making rock dolls 7. Drawing pictures

What Can You Make?

The materials on the left can all be used to make different toys. The toys on the right were all made from everyday things you can find in your house or yard. Can you match the materials on the left with the toys that they can be made into? If you use your imagination you can think of many different toys that you can make for yourself.

Paper, string, sticks

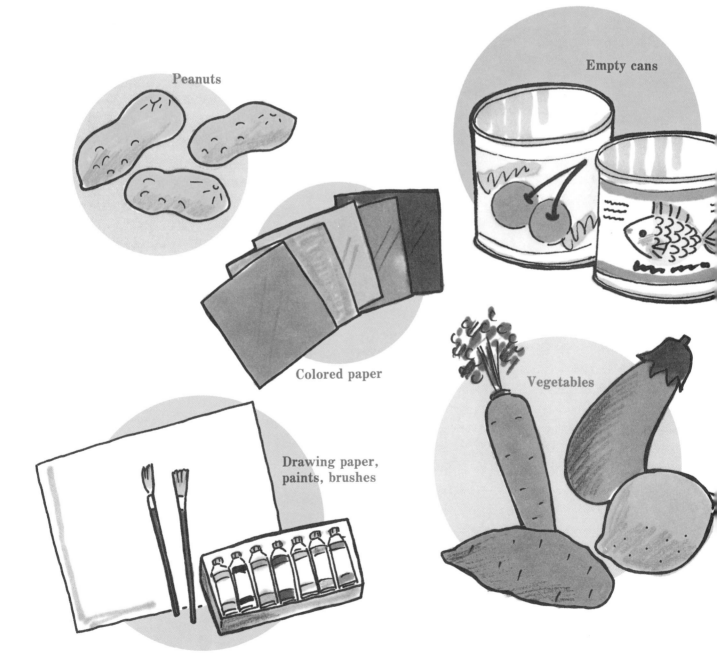

Peanuts

Empty cans

Colored paper

Vegetables

Drawing paper, paints, brushes

Rocks

Modeling clay and tools

1 Stilts	2 Finger puppets
3 Mobile	4 Animal
5 Plane, crane	6 Picture
7 Sculpture	8 Bird

1. Empty cans 2. Peanuts 3. Paper, string and sticks 4. Vegetables 5. Colored paper 6. Drawing paper, paints and brushes 7. Modeling clay and tools 8. Rocks

When Is It Used?

On this page are pictures of objects that you use.
On the page to the right you see children using
these things. Can you match the things on the left
with their uses on the right? How many of these
things have you and some of your friends ever done?

Music score

Tent

Ball

String

Animal cutout

Puzzle

Kite

Candle

1. Kite 2. Animal cutout 3. Ball 4. Tent
5. String 6. Candle 7. Music score 8. Puzzle

86

1

If there is no wind then this won't fly well. But on a windy day it could stay up in the sky for hours.

2

These children are making shadows on the sidewalk. If you shine a light on this object it will cast a shadow.

3

In this game you throw it at the members of the opposite team. You might also play football with this object.

4

If you go camping it is a good idea to bring this with you to sleep in. It will keep you dry if it rains when you are sleeping.

5

This simple object can be used to make things like a cat's cradle. It is also useful for tying up packages or serving as the wick if you make some candles.

6

When the electricity goes out this is a very useful thing to use so that you can see. But you should be very careful because it can also be very dangerous.

7

This is used when playing a song on the piano. It tells you what notes to play and how many beats you should play them for.

8

If you put all these shapes together you will see the picture. But before all the pieces are together you can't tell what it is.

A Child's First Library of Learning

Things to Do

Time-Life Books Inc. is a wholly owned subsidiary of
The Time Inc. Book Company
Time-Life Books, Alexandria, Virginia
Children's Publishing

Publisher:	Robert H. Smith
Managing Editor:	Neil Kagan
Associate Editors:	Jean Burke Crawford
	Patricia Daniels
Marketing Director:	Ruth P. Stevens
Promotion Director:	Kathleen B. Tresnak
Associate Promotion Director:	Jane B. Welihozkiy
Production Manager:	Prudence G. Harris
Editorial Consultants:	Jacqueline A. Ball
	Andrew Gutelle
	Sara Mark

Editorial Supervision by:
International Editorial Services Inc.
Tokyo, Japan

Editor:	C. E. Berry
Associate Editor:	Winston S. Priest
Translation:	Joseph Hlebica
	Bryan Harrell
Writer:	Pauline Bush
Editorial Staff:	Christine Alaimo
	Nobuko Abe

Cover:	Roger Foley

TIME LIFE ®

Library of Congress Cataloging in Publication Data
Things to do.

    p.   cm.—(A Child's first library of learning)
    Summary: Instructions for making such challenging
projects as seashell mobiles, peanut puppets, paper airplanes,
and vegetable animals, presented in a question and answer
format.
    ISBN 0-8094-4897-1   ISBN 0-8094-4898-X (lib. bdg.)
    1. Handicraft—Juvenile literature. 2. Handicraft—
Miscellanea—Juvenile literature. [1. Handicraft. 2. Questions
and answers.] I. Time-Life Books. II. Series.
TT157.T47 1989   745.5—dc20   89-20426

Fourth printing 1993. Printed in U.S.A.
Published simultaneously in Canada.

TIME-LIFE is a trademark of Time Warner Inc. U.S.A.

Time-Life Books Inc. offers a wide range of fine publications,
including home video products. For subscription information,
call 1-800-621-7026 or write TIME-LIFE BOOKS, P.O. Box
C-32068, Richmond, Virginia 23261-2068.